HAMID'S STORY...

A real-life account of his journey from Eritrea

Created by
Andy Glynne
Illustrated & designed by
Tom Senior

This paperback edition published in 2016 by Wayland
First published in hardback in 2014
Text and Illustrations © Mosaic Films 2014

Wayland, Carmelite House, 50 Victoria Embankment EC4Y 0DZ

Mosaic Films, Shacklewell Lane, London E8 2EZ

Created by Andy Glynne
Illustrated and designed by Tom Senior

Editor: Debbie Foy
Layout design: Sophie Wilkins

Dewey ref: 362.7'7914'092-dc23

ISBN 978 0 7502 9281 8
eBook ISBN 978 0 7502 9348 8
Lib eBook ISBN 978 0 7502 7895 9

Printed in China

10 9 8 7 6 5 4 3 2 1

Wayland is a imprint of Hachette Children's Group,
An Hachette UK company.

www.hachette.co.uk
www.hachettechildrens.co.uk

HAMID'S
STORY...

My name is Hamid.

This is the story of my
journey from Eritrea.

WAYLAND
www.waylandbooks.co.uk

When my family and I were living in Eritrea,
it was always so hot and busy.

There were lots of street markets in our town where people sold many different types of food.

It was so hot
at the markets
that the food
would have flies
swarming all
over it.

And the streets were
so dusty that when
the wind blew, you
would end up with
lots of dust in
your eyes.

Eritrea is a small country but lots of people live there, so the buses were always packed full. We usually had to stand up as there weren't enough seats for everyone.

Even babies had to give up their seats to allow an older person to sit down. It could be quite dangerous for them.

Red Sea

Eritrea

Ethiopia

A long time ago Eritrea used to be
a big country, but then the land was
divided between Eritrea and Ethiopia.

When Eritrea split from
Ethiopia, Eritrea's border was
next to the Red Sea.

The war started because Ethiopia
decided they wanted the Red Sea!

The Eritrean people wanted to escape
the war, but it was difficult to get a
flight out of the country.

Many people fled Eritrea to try and
find somewhere safe for themselves
and their families.

My dad knew some secrets about the Eritrean government. The officials said that if he told anyone these secrets then they would kill my mum and me!

So dad told us we had to run away.
He couldn't come with us because
the government wouldn't let
him leave the country.

My mum and I boarded a plane.
All I can remember is that we travelled for
a very, very long time.

For part of our journey we took a bus.
I slept a lot of the way.

Finally, we arrived in our new country.
It was really difficult for us at first because
we didn't speak the language.

I started school. It was really scary because
I didn't have any friends and all of the
other kids were already in groups.

One day in the playground a boy asked me if
we could be friends. We started playing together
and then, after a little while, we joined in
with lots of the other kids.

Soon we'd made a new group of friends.

A few weeks later I arrived home from
school to find lots of ladies in my
house. Everyone was crying.

I went upstairs to my mum's room
and she was sitting on the bed.
'I have something to tell you,'
she said. 'Your dad has died
back home in Eritrea.'

We both got really upset. After a little while, we
told each other we must be strong, and

For a few days I could hardly eat anything.
I drank a little bit of water but couldn't
finish my lunch at school.

The next day my mum spoke to me.

She explained that I shouldn't be so upset because,
in the end, the reason why we left Eritrea was
because it was so dangerous.

I began to feel much better after our chat. I realised that it was a good thing that we had left Eritrea and come to this new country.

I've made a lot of new friends, but we don't talk about our lives at home. We act like sad things have never happened to us.

So when I'm feeling sad, my friend tells me a joke
and cheers me up. And when he's feeling sad,
I tell him a joke and cheer him up.
Life is much better for us now...